TRACKS A
TRACKLESS
CHESTERFIELD'S TRAMS
AND TROLLEYBUSES

GW01417635

TRACKS AND TRACKLESS
CHESTERFIELD'S TRAMS AND TROLLEYBUSES

Barry M. Marsden

AMBERLEY

First published 2012

Amberley Publishing
The Hill, Stroud
Gloucestershire, GL5 4EP

www.amberley-books.com

British Library Cataloguing in Publication Data.
A catalogue record for this book is available from the British Library.

ISBN 978 1 4456 0536 4

Typeset in 10pt on 12pt Sabon.
Typesetting and Origination by Amberley Publishing.
Printed in the UK.

Contents

Introduction

I was born and brought up in Chesterfield and as a child lived for many years opposite the Thornfield Depot of the Corporation Transport Department which replaced the old tram depot on Chatsworth Road in 1927 after the changeover from trams to trolleybuses. Over the last thirty years I have written a number of books on various tram and trackless systems in northern England, but those of my native town have always exercised the deepest fascination. This book is intended as a pictorial journey, and those interested in a more thorough history of the undertaking can always consult my other works on the subject. Like the data for the history, the photographs have been collected over many years from a variety of sources. Fortunately, two precious relics of the tramway era still survive at Crich Tramway Museum: Horse Car 8 and Electric Car 7, the former rescued as a summerhouse in the 1930s and renovated locally in the 1980s, the latter as a holiday home at Two Dales, and restored in the 1990s. I hope that readers may find as much pleasure in reading this history, and enjoying its many often rare photographs, as I had in compiling it.

Barry M. Marsden
Eldwick, January 2012

A Brief History of the System
(1882–1938)

Established as a Roman settlement *circa* AD 55, Chesterfield sits on a low hill above the confluence of the rivers Hipper and Rother. Located on the Coal Measures, mining was once the principal occupation of the male workforce. At the time of the trams no less than three railways served the township, providing an excellent communications network. Chesterfield was the first English town to illuminate its streets with electricity, in 1881, and by the early 1900s was home to a number of flourishing industries. Its population was 27,000 in 1901, a figure which had more than doubled by 1921.

Chesterfield has an interesting transport history as it deployed a series of early urban transit vehicles, including horse trams, electric trams, trolleybuses and motorbuses. The horse cars were inaugurated by the Chesterfield and District Tramways Company, founded in 1879 but not viable until November 1882. Despite a number of proposed lines, the only track constructed was a mile-long stretch of standard gauge from Low Pavement westwards to Walton Lane, with a tramshed at Rodney Yard. Three trams were provided, including two Eade's reversible double-deckers and a single-decker. The company operated on a shoestring basis for some three years before going into liquidation with debts of £500.

A new body, the Chesterfield Tramways Company, took over in December 1886, and in 1890 increased the car fleet with two more single-deckers. In 1897 the Corporation purchased the undertaking and bought a sixth car, another single-decker. Two more single-deckers joined the fleet as the facility flourished, all painted in a livery of Prussian blue and white, and No. 8 is preserved at Crich as a permanent exhibit. In 1903 the Corporation added a further double-decker, bought from Sheffield at the knockdown price of £5, but in view of the now worn-out trackway, it is doubtful if the conveyance ever ran. Robert Acland, the new electrical engineer, was given the task of organising the electrification of the line and extending it westward to the borough boundary, and northward through the town and out as far as Whittington Moor. The line, single track with turnouts, and doubled through the narrow town centre, was commenced in August 1904 and finished by November. It was 3 5/8 miles long, with a town terminus at Low Pavement and a facing crossover at Cavendish Street when the facility was operated as two separate sections at weekends. A new tramshed and offices were built on Chatsworth Road, erected by departmental staff.

The rolling stock consisted of twelve Brush open-toppers painted in carmine red and primrose. They were of standard pattern but boasted state-of-the-art Brush Radial trucks of an 8 foot, six inch wheelbase, promising a steadier ride and some flexibility on curves. There was no opening ceremony, and the line was opened in stages from 20 December until the end of January 1905. In the first few years the undertaking was viable, though running costs always kept pace with revenue. In 1907, two more trams joined the fleet, running this time on Brush Flexible Axle trucks. In 1909, Acland ordered a Brush water car, No. 15, built to his specification and mounted on a long wheelbase truck.

By 1909, faults were becoming apparent on the track, with wear on the curves and loop points, and receipts failed to improve due to static passenger figures and original loans spread over too long a period. Components aged long before initial optimistic forecasts of their longevity, and tramways which had operated on bare profits encountered increasing deficits as track, trams and overhead needed more and more attention. In 1914 three Brush balcony cars were added to the rolling stock, running on Peckham P22 Pendulum trucks on an 8 foot wheelbase. The war caused an urgent shortage of manpower and materials, exacerbated by a severe fire in October 1916 which gutted the tramshed and badly damaged several vehicles. Car 17 was completely rebuilt and No. 7 was restored with a top-cover. By 1919 Cars 6, 8, 11 and 12 had also been retrospectively roofed.

By 1920, the condition of the tramway was causing serious concern. Track and trams were kept serviceable by patching-up exercises, but by 1924 the Corporation was determined on trolleybus replacement. This took place in 1927 when the overhead was converted, and on 23 May Car 14, suitably bedizened, undertook a final run from Cavendish Street to Whittington and back to the depot before trolleybuses opened the new service later that day. In the 1990s, Car 7, purchased as a holiday home in 1927 and located above Two Dales, was restored at Crich, where it now runs regularly.

Chesterfield had flirted with trolleybuses in 1912, with the idea of connecting the town with several outlying districts, but the proposal was killed off by the war. Tramways Manager Walter Marks was responsible for the 1927 trolleybus replacement, and he ordered fourteen Straker-Clough single-deckers in a livery of Suffield green and white. In September a new depot and offices at Thornfield, Stonegravels was opened to house the new trackless and motorbus fleet, and in October proposals were set afoot to open eight new trolleybus routes, similar to the 1912 scheme. Ultimately, however, only one new trackless route, to New Whittington, was sanctioned and this opened in July 1929, extending the total electric route mileage to five.

In 1931, the fleet was augmented by two cutting-edge Ransomes D2 double-deckers, which began operating that December, purchased to cope with increasing passenger traffic, and in late 1935 three single-deck Karrier-Clough E4s, from the defunct York system, increased the fleet to nineteen (Straker 13 had been redesignated 15 in 1929). Four demonstrators had also spent time under Corporation wires between 1928 and 1936, mainly from the Leyland Company. Though the trolleybuses were an undoubted success during their short working lives, end-to-end rewiring became essential in 1938, and a new sub-station was needed to cope with the increased load. These factors, plus an increase in electricity charges, led manager Richard Hoggard to opt for the cheaper oil omnibus, though the increasing threat of war might have suggested caution. In the event, a still-newish trolleybus fleet, powered by electricity produced from local coal, would perhaps have remained a more sensible option. In the event, the vehicles were phased out on 24 March 1938 after a terminal run by Nos 8 and 20, suitably bedecked in valedictory trappings, along the whole system.

The trolleybuses had, during their short lives, not only paid off the old tram debts in full but also the road reinstatement after the removal of the rails, plus their own purchase costs. Their quietness and the environmentally friendly nature of their motive power would be greatly missed in the face of the more noisy and noxious motorbus!

The Horse Trams
(1882–1904)

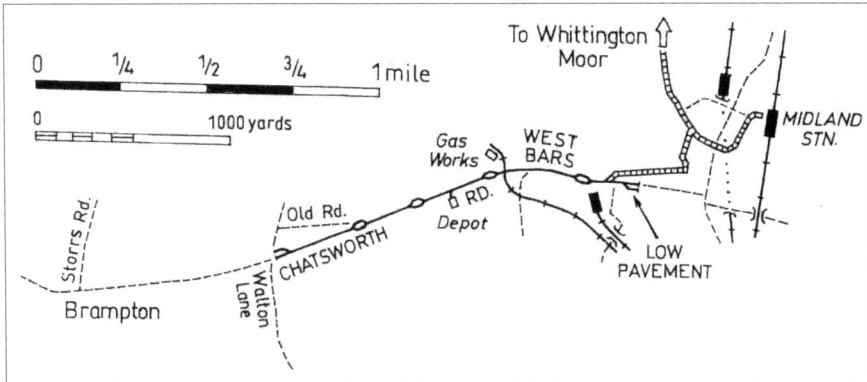

The Chesterfield Horse Tramway as inaugurated in 1882 was a much emasculated remnant of a far more ambitious scheme intended to link Brampton and Whittington with the town centre. In the event it was merely a mile-long single line-and-loop trackway running west from Low Pavement to Walton Lane (after R. Smith).

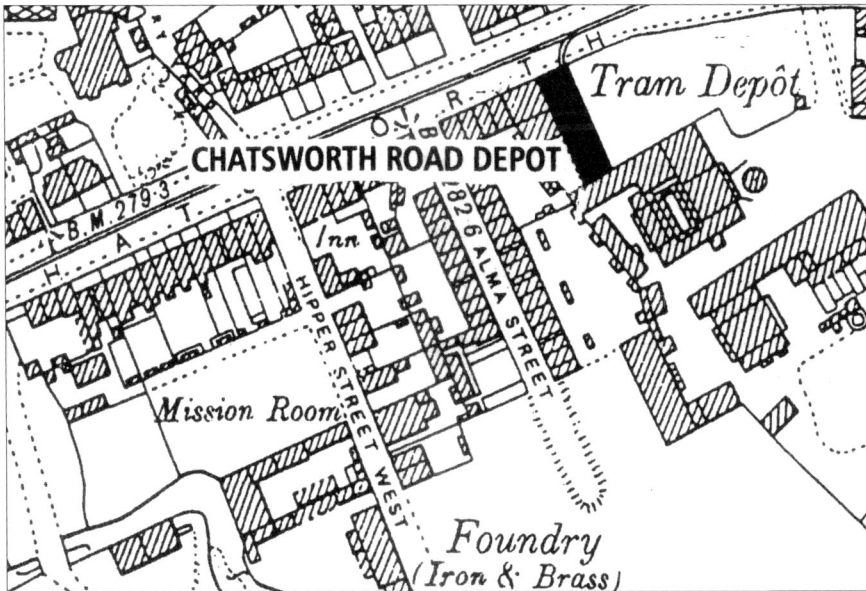

The original tramshed was in Rodney Yard, and access to the main line was via a single track directing vehicles towards town.

A dire print, but of interest as it shows the horse tram crews at the depot in the early 1900s. Inspector Francis Root is the lavishly moustached and uniformed individual on the back row in front of a line-up of 6-8 class cars. Second from left, back row is Seth Hall and second left front row his son Horace, both later electric tram motormen. The dapper gent in the bowler is driver Ezra Coates.

The town terminus for the horse cars was Low Pavement, at the south end of the Market Place. Here, Car 2 is pictured turning on its patent Eade's truck, the side-stepping horses swinging the car body round on its rigid axis for the journey to Walton Lane. This type of truck held a lighter body as only one staircase was needed.

A bird's-eye view of the terminus, looking west, shows a single-deck car awaiting passengers. The building on the right is the Market Hall, an imposing edifice completed in 1857.

A unique shot of one of the 5-6 Milnes single-deckers supplied to the tramway in 1890 standing at Low Pavement. Colours are unknown, but the fancy lining-out included the fleet number, 5, in a garter. The company name is likewise ornately rendered, and advertising boards adorn the roof line.

Single-deck Car 7 is shown bathed in afternoon sunshine at Low Pavement as a passenger boards at the rear entrance. Two horses haul the conveyance, and the car interior boasts curtains. The driver is Seth Hall, the conductor his son Horace.

Eade's boxy-looking double-deck No. 1 stands in the same place with an attendant crowd of youngsters. The lower saloon is well patronised, but the open upper deck remains empty.

Single-deck Car 8 poses at Low Pavement in front of Tyler's boot and shoe emporium. It is pulled by a pair of horses, and Ezra Coates, the driver, is accompanied by a youthful conductor. The livery was Prussian blue and white.

Taken from the Market Hall looking west, this unique view shows the tramline on the extreme left, heading towards West Bars with a car approaching in the distance. New Square still houses the weekly markets and the structure at bottom right is a horse-cab shelter.

MARKET HALL, CHESTERFIELD

Looking in the opposite direction, this image shows the tram track coming out of Low Pavement on its way to Brampton. The previous picture must have been taken from an upstairs window of the Market Hall.

Nearing the end of its townward journey, one of the Eade's double-deckers halts by the Sun Inn on the left, with the new Portland Hotel on the right. Note the single staircase and the knifeboard seating on the top deck of the tram. Crowds suggest a busy market day Saturday.

In a leafy West Bars the entrance to West House, erstwhile home of Lady Baden-Powell, can be glimpsed on the right. Car 8 passes a companion vehicle on the loop, while a number of horse carts occupy the right-hand thoroughfare.

Ezra Coates directs Car 8 again, further west on a muddy West Bars, with the entrance to Clarence Road visible behind the tram. On this day a single horse supplies the motive power.

Probably the oldest picture in the book, this view of Eade's Car 2 shows it posed outside the Square and Compass pub on West Bars. A juvenile conductor obscures the fleet number while the lack of advertising and rocker panel lining-out suggest a pre-1897 date, before the Corporation takeover.

Eade's Car 1 moves steadily up Chatsworth Road at a sedate two miles an hour sometime around 1900, with the entrance to Brook Yard on the left, and the Masons' Arms on the far right. The visible buildings still stand today.

Eade's Car 2 pauses at the junction with Walton Lane, western terminus for the horse trams. Again a young conductor is serving on the conveyance, and the track ends can be seen behind the horses' rear hooves. This spot is now a busy roundabout.

The Scott Postcard Company retailed many cards, firstly commemorating the demise of horse-car transport, then celebrating their replacement by new electric systems. Here the passing of Chesterfield's undertaking is marked by the picture of Car 2 turning at Low Pavement.

In
Affectionate Remembrance
— of the —
Chesterfield Horse Cars

"The last turn of the old Tram."

Which succumbed to an

— Electric Shock —

December 19th, 1904,

After many years of faithful Service,

"Gone, but not forgotten."

"Scott" Series 346.

Another Scott money-spinner was the 'Old and New Car' theme, nicely exploited in this view of Electric Car 9, on its initial trial, meeting Horse Car 7 on the turnout by the new tram depot on a marshy stretch of roadway.

CHESTERFIELD NEW AND OLD TRAMS

The theme is again demonstrated as Coates' Horse Car 8 meets Electric Car 7 on the St Thomas's loop, opposite Stewart's Tailors at 480 Chatsworth Road, on a rainy day. The horse cars of course never ran as far west. This view was replicated at Crich Tramway Museum in 1997, though Car 7 was then top-covered.

Horse Car 8 was preserved at Chesterfield's Thornfield Depot on Sheffield Road after serving as a garden shed. This image shows the interior of the conveyance sometime in the 1930s.

After several refurbishments the little tram finally made its way to Crich, where it appears here running wrong line on a 1980s open day. The car is now a static exhibit at the museum.

Laying the Electric Tramlines (1904)

Taken in the same location as No. 20, and looking west with St Thomas' Church on the right, this shot highlights the short-term problems caused by tracklaying during the late summer of 1904. Piled spoil covers the left side of the road, leaving only a narrow access ribbon on the right.

The entrance to the new tramshed on Chatsworth Road included a lengthy turnout with a 'Y' junction taking trams west and east onto the main line. Workmen and idlers are here controlled by a solitary policeman, and a baby-in-arms is paraded for the camera.

The complicated trackwork at the entrance shows up well in this official photograph which embodies the British Helsby contractor's advertising board on the left. This work was in progress by October, observed by the usual sightseers.

The tram depot loop, looking east, shows the junction in the middle distance and illustrates again the difficulties the tracklaying must have caused to Chatsworth Road traffic.

By October operations had moved to the town centre, and this view shows navvies laying twin tracks at the eastern end of New Square, by the Market Hall Coffee Rooms. The white board lists the café menu.

LAYING ELECTRIC TRAMWAY CHESTERFIELD

The camera looks along High Street as operations closed off the town centre for six weeks, to the chagrin of the local shopkeepers. Though the rails are being positioned, the bracket poles still lack their bowstrings and running wire. The usual idlers gather to watch lesser mortals toil!

LAYING ELECTRIC TRAMWAY BURLINGTON ST. CHESTERFIELD

Further east along Burlington Street, the lines push through the town's main thoroughfare. The vista gives a good sighting of a variety of Edwardian shop frontages. Note the ornate lamps suspended from the tips of the bracket poles, which now boast their bowstring supports.

At the east end of the street, the track begins its 48-foot radius curve into Stephenson Place (then called Knifesmithgate). It was the sharpest bend on the whole line. Concrete has already been laid between the rails and the usual urchins pose on the cross-street planks.

More loungers, mostly well-dressed, display deep interest in proceedings as workmen apply the finishing touches to the facing crossover at the entrance to Cavendish Street.

Another view of the crossover, seen here with the rails heading down Cavendish Street. The layout enabled trams to stand side-by-side at weekends, when no cars were allowed through the busy town centre. Again, chaos reigned supreme while the rails were laid.

Lower down the street, at an earlier stage in the proceedings, labourers busily excavate the road under the gaze of bemused townsfolk. The photograph again emphasises the disruption caused by the arrival of tramways in towns.

The tracklaying here approaches Holywell Cross, a much run-down area of the town judging by the buildings on the right.

An opposite view shows the same street under siege as the twin tracks near Holywell Cross. A variety of goods, edible and otherwise, adorn the shop windows, though the hanging poultry would promote heart failure in a modern health inspector!

A wintry scene at the entrance to Sheffield Road, with Holywell House on the right, as the through-town rails are linked with the single track coming south from Whittington. A policeman regulates the disorder as the blocked-off roadway obviously necessitated a traffic detour north via Newbold Road to the left.

Another well-posed official image, dating from August, as the British Helsby workforce construct the Holy Trinity loop just below Holywell House. The setts on the right are ready for laying, and a motley group of navvies and spectators are posed on the left. The crumbling wall behind them was soon to be rebuilt as the frontage to the new girls' grammar school.

Inauguration of the Electric Tramway (December 1904)

Robert Lawford Acland (1872–1937), Chesterfield's first electrical engineer and tramways manager, was the chief architect of the system, planning the route and overseeing its progress for some fifteen years.

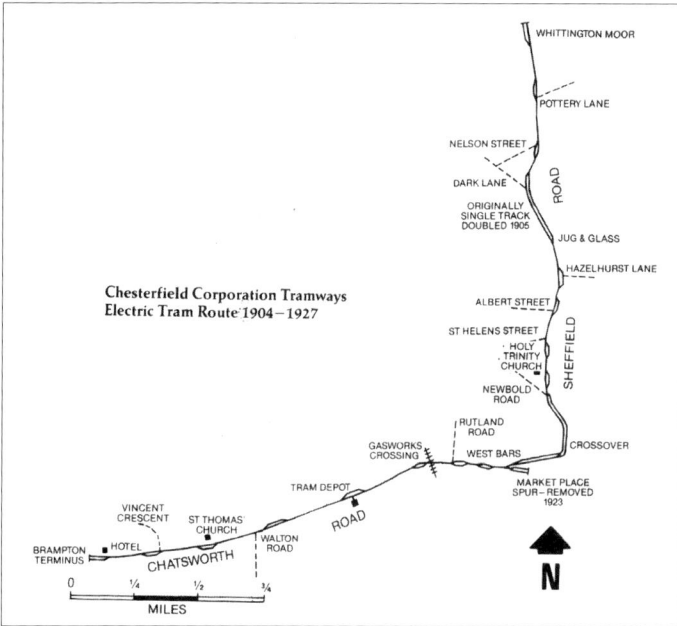

Chesterfield Corporation Tramways
Electric Tram Route 1904–1927

WHITTINGTON MOOR
POTTERY LANE
NELSON STREET
DARK LANE
ORIGINALLY SINGLE TRACK DOUBLED 1905
JUG & GLASS
HAZELHURST LANE
ALBERT STREET
ST HELENS STREET
HOLY TRINITY CHURCH
NEWBOLD ROAD
RUTLAND ROAD
CROSSOVER
GASWORKS CROSSING
WEST BARS
MARKET PLACE SPUR – REMOVED 1923
TRAM DEPOT
VINCENT CRESCENT
ST THOMAS CHURCH
WALTON ROAD
BRAMPTON TERMINUS
HOTEL
CHATSWORTH ROAD
SHEFFIELD ROAD

0   ¼   ½   ¾
MILES

N

The tram route, some 3 5/8 miles long, ran from the western borough boundary at Brampton to Whittington Moor to the north. It was mainly single-line and loop with twin tracks through the town centre and along part of Sheffield Road.

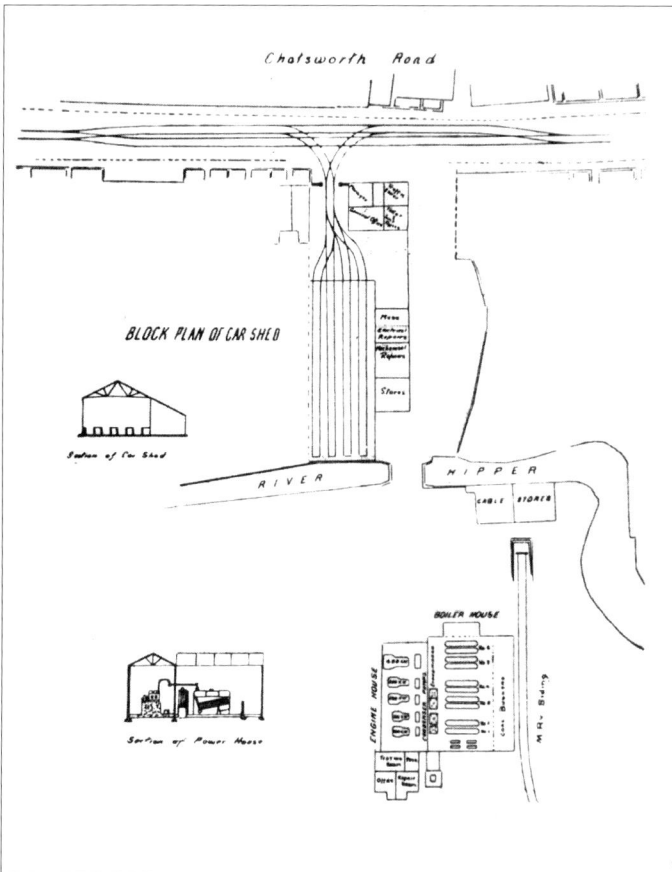

Chatsworth Road

BLOCK PLAN OF CAR SHED

Section of Car Shed

RIVER   HIPPER

CABLE STORES

BOILER HOUSE

ENGINE HOUSE

M.R. SIDING

Section of Power House

The new tramshed fronted Chatsworth Road. It was originally constructed to house sixteen cars on four tracks set over inspection pits.

The shed itself was erected by departmental staff. It was brick-built with a slate roof and measured 126 by 26 feet. It was enlarged in 1914 to cater for cars 16–18, and is one of the few early transport artefacts to survive in the town.

The tram that never was! Shopkeeper Josiah Taylor produced this advertising card to promote both his emporium and the new cutting-edge transport. Sadly, everything about this vehicle is wrong, including the three-window saloon, reversed staircases and the highly speculative lettering. The image obviously represents an existing vehicle that has been carefully doctored by a professional photographer!

Pulled by a team of straining horses, the body of Car 7 rolls onto Chatsworth Road by the Barrel Inn seen in the background. The tram bodies were unloaded from flat cars at the nearby Factory Street siding of the Midland Railway. The track has been laid, though the appalling state of the road makes this hard to believe!

Another 'Old and New Car' shot lines up Horse Car 8 in front of Electric Car 7 with the Public Refreshment Rooms opposite the tramshed entrance in the background.

Nicely dated to 30 November, the body of Car 10 poses at the same venue as No. 44, with a local constable on crowd control. The overhead is still being strung, and the cable drum on the left contained some half-mile of hard-drawn copper wire.

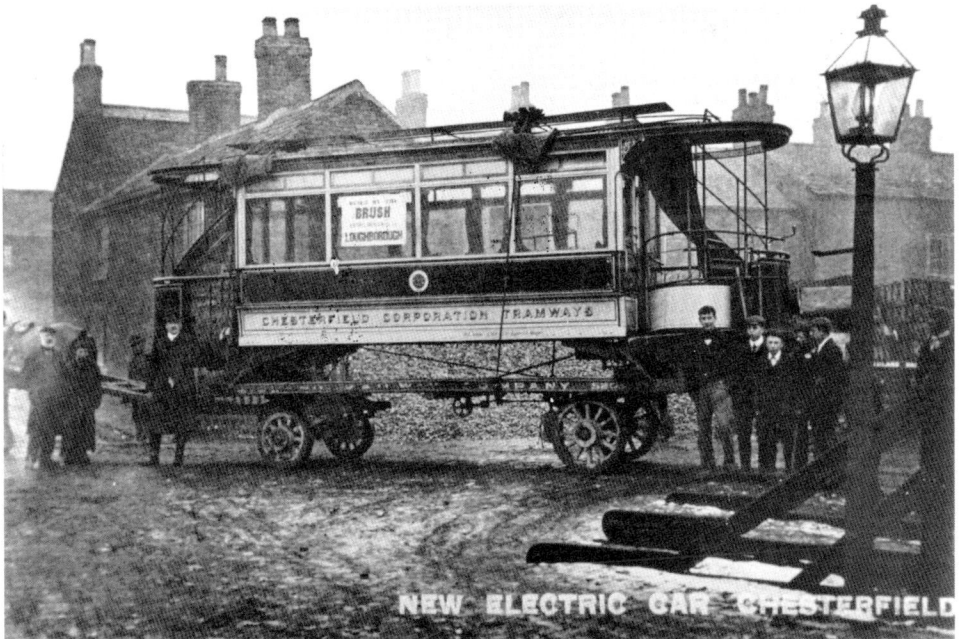

At rest in the depot yard, Car 7 awaits unloading and the fitting of its component parts. The livery, carmine red and primrose, has already been applied, and a Brush Company bill appears in the saloon window.

A fine study of the newly-delivered cars in the tramshed. Car 9, the initial trials vehicle, is fully assembled apart from its upper deck wire mesh. Car 6 sports the netting but no lifeguards, while 7 and 8 are still undergoing construction. A line of trolley masts can be seen along the left-hand wall.

Newly-completed Car 6, patent brass bar across the front platform, stands in pristine glory in the depot yard, with an admiring crowd on the distant left. The rear of the tramway offices can be seen on the right.

The inaugural trial took place on 3 December and Car 9 can be seen at Brampton terminus, with the Old Pheasant Inn on the right of the vehicle. Tramways Manager Acland mans the controls, with his wife and young child on his left. The passengers consist of Brush Company representatives.

Another view of the trial car outside the depot, with the spectators largely hailing from the nearby Brampton Board School. The main features of the pristine conveyance show up well.

Another excellent view of Car 9 at rest on Chatsworth Road in the vicinity of Hipper Street, on another stretch of muddy thoroughfare. The elderly gent on the left seems supremely indifferent to the example of transport progress passing by.

Car 7 was also involved in the early December trials, in this case on the 6th. The locality is near the last, and the uniformed gent on the platform is Chief Inspector Frank Root, formerly in charge of the horse car fleet.

Another Scott postcard hails the introduction of the new electric trams to the town. This one is of interest as it portrays an actual venue – High Street, with the Crooked Spire in the distance.

Tram crews parade in this fine portrayal which dates from early 1905. They include from left to right, back row: Pickering, Baker, Root, Townsend, Davenport. Third row: Shaw, Coates, Cotterill, Bacon, Birks, Mortimer, Owen, Haw. Second row: Wicks, Hopkinson, Longden, Marshall, Hall, Stubbs, Stone, Wheatley, Lander. Front row: Woodhouse, Boden, Lowe, John Blount, Mellor, James Blount, Turner, Bennett, Kirk.

A splendid side view of one of the new cars at the Brampton terminus, showing the salient points of the conveyances. Of interest are the 8 foot 6 inch wheelbase Brush radial truck and the electric track brake. Adverts already adorn the vehicle, and the saloon window bill for the Theatre Royal nicely dates the image to February 1905.

Car 7, gleaming in its new paint job, is pictured in the sylvan surroundings of Brampton terminus in the first winter of service. The motorman is Charles Marshall.

Car 4 heads up New Square in the first days of tramway operation, moving onto the double track which ran through the town centre. The spur line to the Low Pavement terminus leads off to the right. Stone setts piled by the cab shelter indicate that road paving was still in progress.

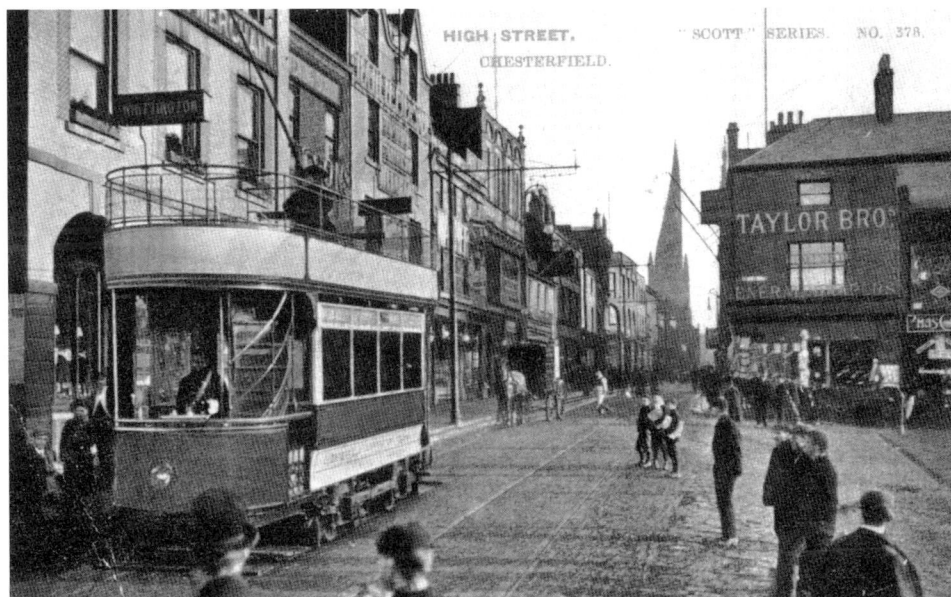

Probably the earliest photograph of electric car operation in town, this view shows a tram (probably No. 4) heading down High Street, almost certainly in the opening week, before Christmas. Note the 'Xmas Card' sign above the Boot's branch on the far right. Compare this image with 53 – the drawing is obviously taken from this postcard, which was franked January 1905.

Images 57–9 must date from the same Scott series. Here, Car 4 poses in the narrow confines of Burlington Street, where the twin rails allowed little room between track and pavement. The driver is Motorman Stone.

Early Years of the Tramway
(1904–1914)

THE CROOKED SPIRE, CHESTERFIELD.

PAT.—" We're not passing that steeple. We're not so dafted as we look."
TRAM DRIVER.—" And, by jove, you don't stand need to be either."

Both the tramway and the Crooked Spire appear in this comic card posted in 1908. Interestingly the location is again recognisable, and the car livery is accurately coloured.

Car 4 waits at Brampton as a lady cyclist passes the twin-track terminations. The Terminus Hotel, newly built in 1906, appears on the left behind the wooden refreshment hut. A time clock can be seen on the right-hand traction post.

Car 7, the most photographed of all fleet vehicles, at rest at the same place in 1910, with an early 'T' model Ford behind it. The motorman is Edwin Bennett, later an inspector, who died at the early age of 37. The conductor is Cyril Marsden.

A young lady with pram poses opposite Car 9 as it awaits passengers for the trip to town, another prewar scene taken by local lensman Charles Nadin, who was responsible for many early twentieth-century images of Chesterfield.

A fine study of the Terminus Hotel, which was sadly demolished by the Council in 2002. Of great interest is Car 13, one of the 1907 additions to the fleet. This is the only known shot of this particular vehicle. Another time clock appears on the tram standard on the left.

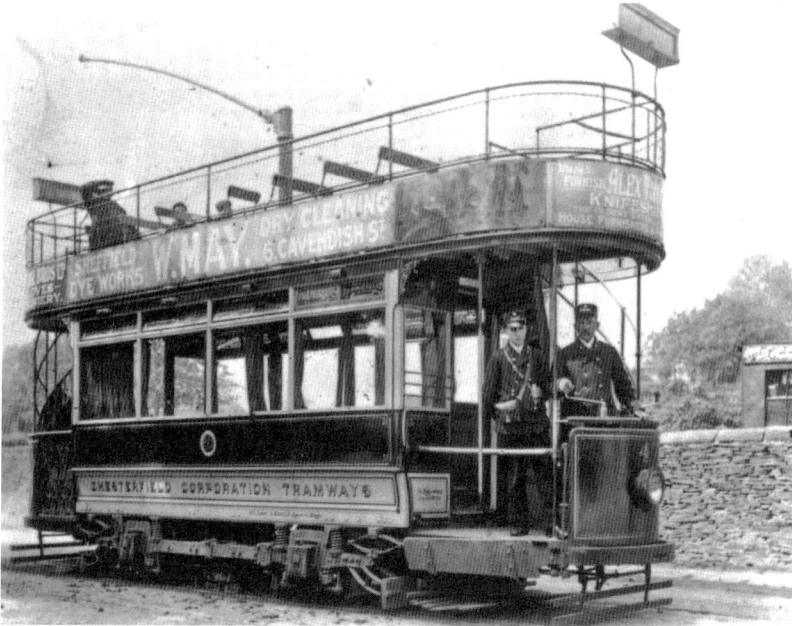

Another good picture of Car 4, with patent brass bar in position, and the crew wearing the kepi-style caps which replaced the earlier peaked ones. The motorman is Cyril Hopkinson, the conductor Derward Lowe. The refreshment hut, doubtless patronised by the tramwaymen, is visible on the right.

From the terminus, the single line headed east along Chatsworth Road. Motive power from here to town was provided by overhead, carried on twin poles and span wire. The youngsters here posing for Nadin's camera near St Thomas' Church would be ill-advised to stand there in today's busy traffic!

MABSIE SERIES. 2.   CHATSWORTH. ROAD

Looking in the opposite direction, Car 1 enters the Vincent Crescent loop on its way to town, following a heavy snowstorm. The fields on the right are now all built over.

CHATSWORTH RD CHESTERFIELD   NADINS SERIES

Just east of Walton Lane, this scene was taken from the upper deck of a tramcar, looking towards town. The overhead lines, passing above the cameraman's head, were raised 21 feet 6 inches above road level. Many of the buildings seen here still survive.

The entrance to the tram depot features the office block fronting Chatsworth Road, with the tramshed to the rear. Note the dash panel propped against the wall behind the gates and the 'Y' junction leading onto the main thoroughfare.

CHATSWORTH RD CHESTERFIELD

In this view Car 1 halts on the gasworks loop, with the Mason's Arms pub on the right. On the left was the extensive premises of the Brampton Brewery, now replaced by a B&Q store. The right-hand buildings have changed little in the 100 or so years since Nadin recorded the scene.

Water Car 15, new in 1909, heads off the West Bars turnout on its way into town, liberally spraying everything in sight from its 2,000-gallon tank. On the left is the entrance to the Park Hotel (formerly West House), with the Market Place railway station on the right.

The little tram is seen here on the Brush Company traverser, minus electrics but with a snow plough fixed to its right-hand end. Boasting an 8 foot 6 inch long wheelbase truck, the car cost £744. A similar vehicle was later provided for the York tramway.

Car 14, new in 1907, heads for the Low Pavement terminus in this busy study of New Square by Dent's Chemist's corner. On Saturdays, trams were barred from the main town thoroughfare due to extreme crowd congestion.

Car 1 proceeds slowly along the Low Pavement single line amid market day stalls and busy shoppers. Take away the tram and overhead and the scene remains much the same today.

A splendid panorama, revealing no less than three cars, Nos 9, 8 and 11, running on the twin track, neatly laid in its bed of limestone setts. The post office stands on the left while to the right rival transport takes time off for a feed. Car 9 is heading for Whittington, though the conductor has failed to reset the destination box.

A well-known image showing Car 7 proceeding along a summer High Street with the Crooked Spire of St Mary and All Saints' Church at the far end of the thoroughfare. A carefully posed little girl stands in the right foreground.

A wide panorama of the upper Market Place as a lightly loaded Car 1 halts on High Street to allow boarders to embark, a scene obviously recorded from an upper room of the Market Hall. The archways, now sadly gone, marked the premises of T. P. Wood, wine and spirit merchant and long-serving councillor, alderman and mayor of the borough.

Two trams slowly rumble past each other along the narrow confines of Burlington Street, dwarfed by the church steeple of St Mary's. The house behind the cars, owned by a Dr Green, was later demolished to construct a short-lived 'Alpine Gardens.'

In this view, Dr Green's abode stands just to the left of Car 4 as it approaches the crossover at the entrance to Cavendish Street, having just negotiated the Burlington Street curve. Knifesmithgate, whose sign adorns the left-hand wall, was then much longer before the eastern end was renamed Stephenson Place after the great railway engineer, who died at Tapton House in 1848.

The figure on the left stands close to where Car 4 rested in the previous photograph. This image looks towards the crossover, where Car 10 awaits passengers for Whittington. Note the sharp curve of the tracks, the imposing automobile on the right and the facade of Deacon's Bank, erected around 1906.

Car 8 halts at the south end of Cavendish Street, accompanied by Nadin's usual crew of posing juveniles. On the right the City House clothing warehouse, with its fine display of lamps, is up for sale. Demolished in 1905, it was replaced by the bank featured in the previous photograph.

At the north end of the street Car 6 takes the curve into the thoroughfare, then dominated by run-down buildings soon to be replaced by Eyre's furniture emporium. The high-roofed Eyre's warehouse, in front of the Crooked Spire, was burned down in 1916. The tram's indicator box still displays 'Whittington' as its destination.

Car 11, pictured at the same stop, by Cooper's confectioners, in a view looking in the opposite direction, the halt indicated by white bands on the traction pole. On the left is Damm's fruiterers, while in the distance another tram can be faintly discerned. The Primitive Methodist Church now serves another purpose.

Looking townwards from further along Holywell Cross, the Crooked Spire looms indistinctly on a misty day. The tramline is still twin-track and the overhead remains supported on bracket poles. Durrant Road descends to the left, while the right-hand area is now occupied by a car park.

The sharp bend at the junction of Newbold Road, on the left, and Sheffield Road occurred just before the rail became single again. Car 10 here climbs the slope on its way into town, while adverts extol various products and the programme at the Corporation Theatre.

Looking the other way from the same vantage point, a tree-lined Holywell Street has the Royal Hospital on the left, while an unidentified tram lurks in the distant shade. Here the tramlines are neatly encased in smooth tarmacadam.

A well-laden Car 2 tackles the incline above the Holy Trinity loop around 1910, with Holywell House just to the distant left of the tram. The fine left-hand wall was built as a frontage to the new girls' grammar school, opened in 1911.

Further down Sheffield Road workmen busily clean out the points at the St Helen's Street turnout. Car 6 lingers on the loop by Day's drapery as passengers embark for town. The tin shack on the left was a nonconformist chapel.

Nadin again used the top deck of a tram for this shot taken by the Albert Street loop, with the track well to the roadside to cater for the bracket poles, which were utilised as far as Whittington. Hardwick Street, seen in front of the lady busily cleaning the pavement, was the future home of the transport department.

The narrow road at the top of Stonegravels hill catered for a double line, with scant room allowed on either side of the track. The derelict pub on the left was the Jug and Glass, demolished in the 1920s. Whittington-bound Car 1 waits by the distant stop sign.

A significant study showing Car 11 also heading for Whittington, an image dating to January–May 1905, before the single track was doubled in order to cut out problems caused by the distant blind bend. The Old Toll Bar Farm can be seen on the left of the picture.

Looking in the opposite direction, Nadin's view reveals that the line has now been doubled as it swings away up Stonegravels hill. Toll Bar Farm, the main subject of the photograph, was demolished after the Second World War.

Manager Robert Acland obscures the fleet number of the approaching tramcar as he checks the doubling of the line, with Dark Lane (now Peveril Road) leading off to the right. This part of the system was then incredibly rural, but is now covered by a busy roundabout.

An interesting tramscape at the northern end of the line, looking up Sheffield Road towards the Whittington Moor terminus. Here, Car 10 moves townwards under a line of bracket poles, with the wall of the Peter Webster School on the right.

Further uphill, the line moves to the roadside as a distant Car 7 leaves the terminus for town. The vista remains much the same today, though without the horse traffic, telegraph poles and tram standards.

A fine study of a special car hired by Whittington baker James Thompson to transport refreshments to the other end of the line for the annual picnic for 2,000 children at Somersall. Thompson appears on the platform in this 1913 scene, and his Belsize van can be seen on the left alongside the water boiler being towed on an old horse car truck. A service car waits at the distant terminus.

Car 7 approaches the terminus along a muddied stretch of roadway, with the Black Horse pub in the background. The tramway was originally scheduled to run some 500 yards further along Sheffield Road, to the left, but in the event was cut back to the Whittington UDC boundary. The fine bracket pole was later replaced by twin poles and span wire.

Car 5, rarely pictured during its service life, stands at the terminus outside Shentall's Cash Stores, owned at the time by the chairman of the Tramways Committee. The usual assortment of bystanders keeps it company.

Looking south from the terminus, this shot picks out the track terminations, with a departing tram visible in the distance. Note that the bracket arms have now given way to twin poles and span wire.

Car 6 has its image recorded for posterity at the 'Moor' sometime before the First World War. The view shows how far the trolley arm has been swung to engage the appropriate wire.

Car 9 waits at the same spot, with building work in progress on the right. The kepi-style crew caps place the picture in the early years of the undertaking. The clumsy-looking destination boxes were abandoned after the First World War.

Corporation trams were available for hire, and this postcard shows one of the fleet parked at the top of the Market Place, appropriately outside Hudson's Music Stores, as the cast of Gilbert and Sullivan's *Mikado*, featuring in a local production, pose for the camera.

Decorated trams featured only rarely in Chesterfield's transport history but in 1910 one of the 13-14 Class cars was dressed for the eight-day September Shopping Festival. The vehicle shows off its plumage on West Bars with a service car behind.

The same conveyance appears in illuminated mode in the depot yard with the crew alongside. The Electricity Department provided the bulbs and wiring, at a cost of £25.

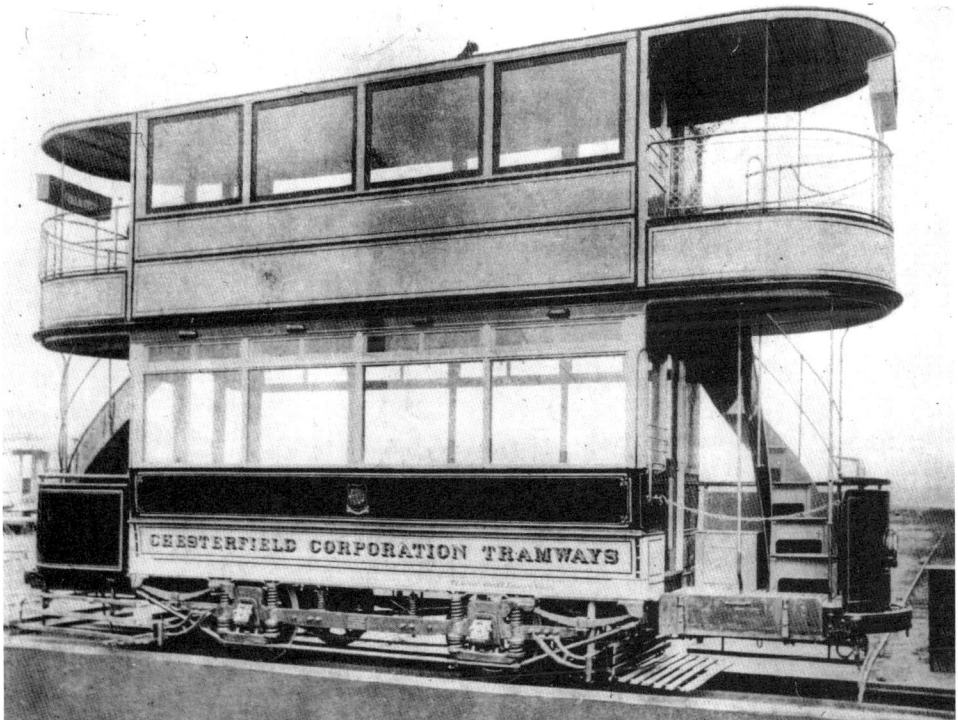

A fine shot of one of the 16-18 Class balcony cars supplied by Brush in June 1914, seen here on the works traverser, minus electrics. Note the new style of lettering and the revised Corporation coat-of-arms, plus the 8-foot Peckham pendulum truck.

Balcony Car 16 as new, pictured on the tramshed loop in the summer of 1914. Motorman Horace Hall, last seen as a youthful conductor in plates 3 and 7, is seen under instruction by Harry Longden, long-term stalwart who drove the last tram when the service closed.

The Tramway at War (1914–1918)

The tramshed as it appeared after the right-hand extension was added in 1914. In this wartime shot Car 17 is seen undergoing complete refurbishment, probably after the October 1916 fire which gutted the depot. A pile of controllers can be seen stacked on the right.

Tramways staff in khaki, obviously on leave with their offspring, are pictured on a visit to the depot in 1917 in front of one of the 1-12 Class conveyances, with a balcony car visible on the right. A patriotic poster adorns the lower saloon window at the top left.

By late 1916 wartime conscription was causing a severe manpower shortage in the department, and female staff were recruited as tram crews. This lineup, posed in front of one of the cars, shows twenty-nine female volunteers who were trained by Chief Inspector Root, seen at centre, second row, Inspector Jimmy Blount (centre right) and Harry Longden (top right).

Again featured in this depot shot, the formidable Inspector Blount is pictured on a car platform with an unidentified motorwoman. Harry Longden is on the right with a youthful trainee on the tram bumper.

Conductress Elizabeth Kneale, who later married Motorman Charles Hopkinson, appears here in front of a 13-14 Class vehicle.

During the war a number of photographs were taken of female staff working on the Corporation's conveyances. Here, rarely pictured Car 5, betraying evidence of hard useage, features Conductress Ellen Burkitt on the platform step.

Elinor Dowson, whose twin sister Emily also served on the trams, here performs under Jimmy Blount's eagle eye on the platform of Car 18. The conductress is Kathleen Allen. The shot is nicely dated by that week's offering at the Hippodrome Theatre, which places it in October 1917.

Millicent Rowbotham 'mans' the controls of Car 18 in this 1918 study, accompanied by Elizabeth Kneale. Millicent was lauded that December when she lessened the impact of a head-on smash on West Bars by braking her car hard. The Tramways Committee awarded her £1 for her cool-headed action.

Car 11 is here pictured at Brampton, driven by Thomas Falconer and sporting a dented dash. The conductress in the fetching headgear remains unidentified.

Another Brampton study, by local photographer Tommy Evans, shows Car 10, with two conductresses, including Ellen Burkitt in civvies, presumably under tuition. Patriotic fare adorns the windows with its usual exhortations for military service.

Balcony Car 17 is the subject of another Brampton scene, again featuring Ellen Burkitt, this time pictured in uniform. A youthful soldier can be seen on an inside seat.

Taken from the opposite direction, with the Terminus Hotel in the background, the omnipresent Ellen again provides the female component of the crew, this time of Car 12.

A fine studio portrait of conductress No. 12, Amy Truman, complete with Bell ticket punch, bag and whistle.

Ann Carline was another wartime conductress, seen here on the platform of an unidentified car. The heavy chain restricting platform entrance was a replacement for the original brass bar. A note on the original print indicates a December 1917 date.

A sunny day at Brampton as Motorman Falconer poses at the controls of Car 9 with an unknown conductress. The inspector is William Cotterill, not the most popular of the department's senior staff, with a proprensity for fisticuffs with both passengers and fellow tramway personnel.

Falconer appears here with a trainee male driver and another conductress at Brampton. Note the patriotic window poster advertising five shilling war bonds to help 'crush the Hun.' A fine ground-glass Lipton's Tea advert adorns the sliding door to the lower saloon.

The Tramway Post-War (1918–1927)

By 1919, younger men were returning to the undertaking as motormen, though women remained on the trams until the end of 1921. Here, Car 17 waits at Whittington shortly after the war with its mixed crew.

Husband and wife team John and Agnes Woodhouse crew Car 16 at Brampton. The tethered rope for swinging the trolleyboom can be seen above George's head. Not so apparent is the reason for the sprig of flowers in his cap!

A caricature of the new Tramways Committee Chairman, Philip Robinson, as it appeared in a 1920 local magazine. Robinson, a 'new broom', was responsible for the changeover from trams to trolleybuses in 1927.

A memorable shot of Car 12 at Brampton in 1920 after receiving a top cover. The tram carries the new Corporation coat of arms and distinctly non-standard lettering on the rocker panel. The motorman is Jack Gretton, the conductress Elizabeth Kneale.

Car 6 was also top-covered post-war. It poses at Brampton, bearing a somewhat weathered appearance. The original neat lettering has now been replaced with larger black characters. The motorman is Jack Rouse, the conductor Gary Gascoyne.

Car 4 at Brampton in a picturesque setting and deplorable looking condition. By this time the indicator boxes had been replaced with boards fixed in the lower saloon windows, and the conductress was soon to be replaced by a male counterpart. This tram was phased out of service in October 1925 after an accident.

Car 14 was seriously damaged in the depot fire of October 1916 and was subsequently rebuilt with an added top cover. The electrics were upgraded at the same time, with T1 controllers replacing the smaller 90Ms. The conductor is Tommy Baker.

On 7 August 1922, flash floods inundated Chatsworth Road as the River Hipper overflowed. Here, one of the balcony cars is stranded below Barker Lane, with the Congregational Church visible on the left, as rising waters brought the service to a standstill.

New Square *circa* 1923, with Car 16 pausing by the Portland Hotel on its way to Brampton. In the foreground the single line opens out into twin track for the through-town route. The wear and tear on the rails at this point can be appreciated.

Car 16 grinds up the incline from New Square onto High Street on its way to Whittington sometime in the early 1920s. The absence of stalls shows it to be a non-market day. By this time both track and vehicles were in an unsatisfactory condition, and the council were considering alternative transport options.

Car 17 at Brampton, now with a post-war all-male crew. The indicator boxes have disappeared and the advertising boards are more discreet than in earlier views.

A woeful print taken on the Cavendish Street crossover, but interesting as it shows the same car with crew and other staff in new uniforms with 'maternity jacket'-style tunics, military-type riding breeches and polished leggings. A Bristol motorbus waits behind the tram.

Serious accidents on the tramway were mercifully rare but on 13 August 1926 a motorcycle ridden by John Mather swerved to avoid a woman near the Rutland Road loop and skidded into Car 17, waiting on the turnout. He later died in hospital, while his passenger Ernest Wallace suffered serious injuries. This photograph records the dismal scene on that unlucky Friday.

Another crash, with less serious consequences, was this incident when Car 8 paid an unscheduled call on Watson's butchers on Stonegravels on 18 October 1926. The tram broke an axle and jumped the Albert Street loop, but was mercifully held upright by the traction pole. Four people were injured, including the motorman, Falconer. Of interest are the STOP sign on the pole, the destination boards in the saloon window and the black lettering on the rocker panel of the stranded vehicle.

May 1927 and the conductor swings the trolleyboom of Car 7, waiting on Cavendish Street in preparation for the run to Whittington. By this time the Brampton route had been converted to trolleybus operation and Bristol motorbus No. 30 (RA 441), on the right, was providing a temporary service along this stretch.

The Trolleybus Era
(1927–1938)

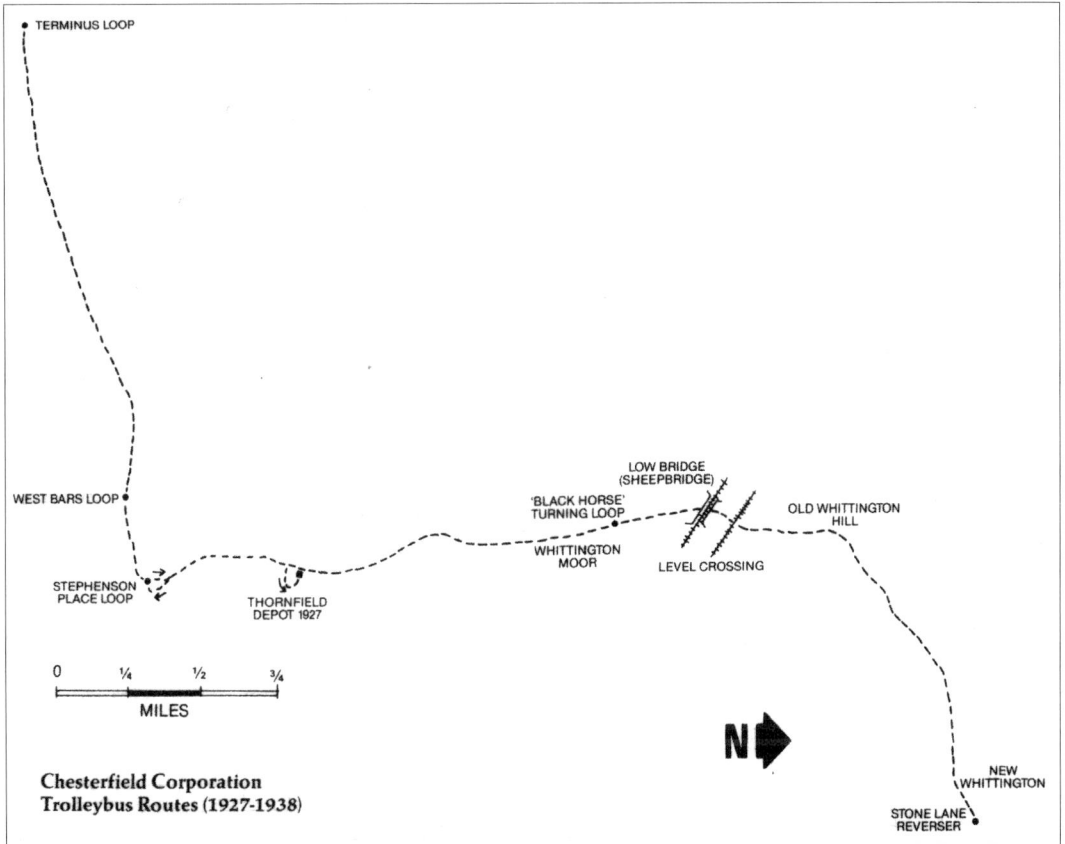

TERMINUS LOOP

LOW BRIDGE
(SHEEPBRIDGE)

'BLACK HORSE'
TURNING LOOP

WEST BARS LOOP

OLD WHITTINGTON
HILL

WHITTINGTON
MOOR

LEVEL CROSSING

STEPHENSON
PLACE LOOP

THORNFIELD
DEPOT 1927

0   ¼   ½   ¾

MILES

N

NEW
WHITTINGTON

**Chesterfield Corporation
Trolleybus Routes (1927-1938)**

STONE LANE
REVERSER

The trolleybus route followed the line of the tramway, with a new depot at Thornfield, Stonegravels. A new one-way system operated down Cavendish Street, along Holywell Cross and up Stephenson Place. In 1929 the wires were extended some two miles to New Whittington, a total length of five miles.

The Trackless Vehicles Sub-Committee (TVSC) are pictured here on an early trial run in Straker-Clough single-decker No. 1 at Brampton terminus. Walter Marks, the new tramways manager, stands in front of the central entrance of the thirty-two-seater, with Robinson on his left.

A fine study of Straker 1 (RA 1810) at the Chatsworth Road depot in its livery of Suffield green and white, taken on 21 April 1927. The vehicle took part in all the early trials on the Brampton–West Bars route. The lettering behind the front wheel indicates its official top speed of 12 mph.

The front (non-smoking) compartment of Straker 5 as seen from the central vestibule. The saloon, whose seats were upholstered, held thirteen passengers. Two further wooden seats were provided in the vestibule, at bottom right. Above the front bulkhead were images of Derbyshire scenery.

The rear (smoking) compartment of Straker 5 provided room for seventeen riders on green leather seating which ran the length of the trolleybus and along the rear.

On 16 May, REV (Railless Electric Vehicle) Straker 1 undertook a test run between West Bars and Brampton, carrying members of the TVSC. Here, the conveyance tests out the West Bars loop on a wet, cheerless day. On the left is Bristol motorbus No. 26 (RB 434), which was providing a temporary service until the deployment of the Strakers.

On 19 May, the same trolleybus took part in official trials under the aegis of the Ministry of Transport. In this view Driver Bill Hardwick tests the manoeuvrability of his charge on the same loop, with the Market Place station on the right. The figure in front of the Straker is probably Lt-Col. G. L. Hall of the MoT, who was in charge of the test.

Another trials shot of Straker 1 heading townwards from Brampton. Note the boom retriever ropes hanging from the trolleyheads, and the tramlines, still *in situ* under the trolleybus wheels.

The ultimate day of tramway operation in Chesterfield, and doesn't it show! The demise of the tramcars is aptly summed up in this scene as Car 14, dented, dilapidated and dirty, and sparsely decorated, arrives at Whittington on its final run on 23 May, bearing the usual *prominenti*. The motorman is Harry Longden, latterly night foreman at the depot.

The Tramways Committee line up in a variety of natty headgear in front of Car 14, bunting whipped by a stiff breeze. Robinson is the tall central figure, with Marks on the extreme right.

The old meets the new at the depot later that day in this memorable shot as Car 14 poses by its replacement, brand-new Straker 1. Robinson is at the head of the lineup of dignitaries, with Marks fourth on his right.

The considerable crowd take a last look at the depot following the terminal ride of Car 14, just visible on the left, with Car 7 behind it. The depot was soon to be abandoned in favour of a newly built complex at Thornfield on Sheffield Road, Stonegravels.

The last official photograph of the day was taken at the Terminus Hotel loop as representatives of the council and transport staff provide the final record of the changeover. Chairman Robinson is standing on the extreme right, with Marks framed in the exit of the Straker.

An aerial view of the new Thornfield premises, a state-of-the-art steel and corrugated iron structure measuring 295 by 150 feet with a floor space of 30,000 square feet, capable of housing 100 vehicles. Trolleybuses travelled down Hardwick Street on the right, entering the depot from the rear. They emerged left front, along the access road behind the offices fronting the main road. The manager's home, Thornfield House, can be seen at top left.

A Straker is seen here parked at the rear of the premises. Trolleybuses entered the back of the vehicle shed via the rather narrow opening seen in the foreground, though the entrance was subsequently widened. The staff clubhouse can be seen on the right with Thornfield House looming behind.

Straker 12 shows off its boxy lines at Brampton during the first summer of service. The lodge on the right was one of a pair lining the entrance to Somersall Lane. It was intended to site a reverser there, but public opposition led to the substitution of the loop visible at the top right.

The Terminus Hotel served as the western boundary of the township's transport for 96 years before its 2002 demolition. Here, Straker 3 pauses on the loop with a group of smartly-uniformed crew members, including Drivers Briggs (left) and Cutts (second right).

In 1934, the trolleybus liveries were revamped, with some lining-out and the Corporation coat of arms replacing the frontal numbers, clearly seen in this view of Straker 12 at Brampton. Note the section box on the right and the hotel on the left.

The only known image of Straker 5, here seen at the terminus in 1936. The Cleveland sign refers to petrol, then retailing at 1s 4d per gallon.

Straker 1 waits at the terminus in the last summer of electric car operation. The photograph details the revised 1934 paint scheme and the wooden latticed lifeguards which prevented pedestrians from falling under the vehicle.

Straker 2 is pictured at Brampton with young Eric Chambers, who scratch-built the model of the REV pictured here, probably the first ever working model of a trolleybus, to the left. John McDonald is the driver, and the diminutive conductor second from right is the author's late uncle, Bill Crampton.

Few shots exist of the Chatsworth Road section of the route. This example, taken looking towards town in 1937 at the junction with Walton Road (now a roundabout), shows Straker 12, trolleys down, probably an innocent bystander in this accident between a Wolseley saloon and a Shentall's van. Along this thoroughfare the overhead was carried on twin poles and span wire. Employees of Pearson's Pottery on the right take a passing interest in the proceedings.

An early study of Straker 4 in sylvan surroundings outside the Park Hotel on West Bars. The Estler trolley housings and long booms show up well against the trees. The redundant tramlines have not yet been removed in this view.

The previous picture was taken just in front of the cyclist seen on the right. The advertising boards put this shot in the summer of 1937. Twin poles and span wire carry the overhead lines, and behind the trees the palatial new town hall is in the process of construction. The Portland Hotel is just in shot on the far right.

Straker 6 heads towards Brampton through an almost deserted New Square in October 1929. The feeder box on the right provides power to the cables supplying the running wire overhead.

Taken late in the trackless era, Straker 7 is shown embarking passengers outside the High Street post office around 1936. The Crooked Spire can be seen in the distance, together with a selection of solid-looking motor cars.

On a quiet Sunday High Street on 5 August 1929, a silent Straker 15 bears down on an unsuspecting motorcyclist. Less than a month earlier the trolleybus bore the number 13, but superstitious crews forced the change! The REV first ran with its new number on 21 July.

This early photograph shows Straker 7 demonstrating its flexibility as it eases past a sporty-looking Vauxhall convertible along a narrow Burlington Street. Trolleybuses had the ability to negotiate other traffic in busy urban situations, one great advantage over the tram.

Straker 11, another rarely sighted REV, poses at the east end of the street in the shadow of the Parish Church. In this animated scene Burton's tailors is offering five-guinea suits for 45s. The shop is still there, but not alas the same bargain!

The Burlington Street corner displays the web of overhead wiring which was such a feature of many townships during the first half of the twentieth century. This locality was allegedly a notorious spot for trolley dewirements, perhaps caused by the sharp bend.

Like Burlington Street, Cavendish Street was rather narrow and, in the face of increased traffic density, trolleybuses were restricted to one-way movement. In this scene, Straker 12, trolleybooms hard over, squeezes past an approaching lorry, itself negotiating a parked car, another image dating to the early 1930s.

Trolleybus traffic approaching from Whittington came back into the town centre via Holywell Street, seen here looking east, with Cavendish Street in the distance to the left. On the right is the Picture House cinema, later renamed the Odeon.

Opposite the Picture House Straker 15 turns off Holywell Street into Stephenson Place in March 1934, a photograph dated by that week's cinema offering, a forgettable British farce called *Up To His Neck*, a title reflected in the side windows of the trolleybus.

An interesting 1930 vista, looking north down Stephenson Place. The web of overhead wires includes the loop for trolleybuses turning right into Cavendish Street on the left, passing round the façade of Deacon's Bank. The mock-Tudor frontage of the Picture House appears in the distance, to the left of the Bristol motorbus waiting at the Staveley stop.

Some seven years on and Straker 8 awaits trade on the right at the Brampton stop. A Titan TD3 double-decker has replaced the Bristol, while the taxi on the left has apparently not moved since the previous image!

A fine 'trolleyscape' at the junction of Newbold and Sheffield roads, with the running wire again supported on twin poles. The roadway is almost deserted, though now the area supports another bustling roundabout. The church is Holy Trinity, where George Stephenson lies buried.

Straker 9, now sporting advertising boards, poses alongside Bristol motorbus RA 4279 outside the hangar-like doors of the Thornfield depot. The trolleybus rather dwarfs its smaller stablemate.

In March 1930, a German transport delegation toured various English systems, visiting Chesterfield on the 23rd. Here the group embark on Straker 12 at Thornfield for a trip to New Whittington. Bowler-hatted manager Richard Hoggard appears on the far right. The line of background houses have long gone, demolished for the new bus depot which opened in 1964.

Street scenes between Thornfield and the Whittington Moor terminus are scant, though this scene shows Sheffield Road at its junction with Pottery Lane, on the right. Note the now-vanished pottery kilns on the left. The overhead is just visible in the photograph, while the hoardings extol both BP Petrol and Camp Coffee.

At the Moor terminus Straker 6 picks up trade for town sometime between 1927 and 1929 before the line was extended to New Whittington. A Bristol motorbus waits by the Black Horse for onward trade to the latter village.

Straker 8 halts by the Queen's Hotel before tackling the turning loop, a photograph postdating the New Whittington extension, whose bracket poles head down Station Road, to the right. At the top of the picture the feeder cables supplying power to the positive trolley wire can just be seen.

In the summer of 1927 a fully-laden and rarely photographed Straker 10 enters the Whittington loop, whose wires, frogs and supporting 'pull-offs' show up well in this image.

A Straker eases round the turning circle on its way to New Whittington in 1937. The Black Horse behind it has now been demolished, and the locality has suffered extensive alterations since this shot was taken.

Two Strakers work the route on either side of the loop, the left-hand one on its way to town, while the nearest pauses on Station Road, picking up riders for New Whittington. The old Lyceum Theatre stands on the left.

Further down Station Road, Straker 2 makes a mandatory stop at the LMS level crossing at the foot of Whittington Hill on its way to a photo session at the New Whittington reverser. The feeder cables, boosting power to the overhead for the steep climb, can be clearly seen. Apparently a too-speedy passage across the rails could result in embarrassing dewirements!

Straker 2 again, its ugly advertising boards marring its roofline, utilises the reverser to back into Stone Lane for the return to town.

Booms in position, Straker 2 waits at the terminus, then a fairly undeveloped locality. The advertising board extols the virtues of 'ROP' – Russian Oil Products.

A revealing view of the 'turning triangle' on Stone Lane as the booms are guided onto the appropriate wires for the return trip. Wellington Street is in front of the REV, while the terrace on the left has been replaced by modern bungalows.

In 1931, the department ordered two state-of-the-art forty-eight-seat Ransomes D2 double-deckers to augment the trolleybus fleet. Here No. 16 poses, trolleys down, at the rear of the depot garage soon after delivery. The vehicles could not deploy beyond Whittington Moor due to the low railway bridge at Sheepbridge.

The graceful lines of its stablemate, Ransomes 17, show up well against the classic ones of the parish church at the Burlington Street corner on 5 December 1931, a run which marked the debut of this advanced trolleybus, three days after its partner.

In this image, taken at Brampton, Ransomes 17 gives a good sighting of its nearside as it negotiates the turning circle which shows up well against the skyline. Note the elegant lines of the Ipswich-built newcomer, which retains the 'piano front' configuration below the front top deck windows.

Ransomes 16 is caught heading townwards by the West Bars loop in this 1934 illustration. On the right is the premises of Charles Nadin, whose lens recorded many aspects of the town in the early twentieth century, including the advent of the trams.

Blurred it may be, but this is one of the few images of a Ransomes in service as No. 17 climbs Stonegravels hill on its way into town in 1937. Stonegravels Lane can be seen on the right, and the large gabled house behind the trolleybus, once the Cleansing Department Offices, has since been demolished.

In late 1935, three ex-York Karrier-Clough E4 thirty-two-seat single-deck trolleybuses joined the electric fleet. This rare photograph catches Karrier 18 at Stephenson Place at the Brampton stop, opposite Deacon's Bank. These up-to-date vehicles only served the township for just over two years.

Views of the Karriers are extremely uncommon, but the late Charles Hall captured No. 19 in New Whittington, moving along High Street with Stone Lane on the right.

Here, Karrier 19 heads towards the Stone Lane reverser, seen overhead, giving a good sight of its rear entrance as the conductor oversees the familiar operation.

Trolleybus Farewell
(23 March 1938)

An evocative view of Karrier 20 leading out Straker 8 on the final day of trolleybus operation. Both buses are suitably bedizened with valedictory trappings, including 'R.I.P' in the destination windows, plus bunting and frontal shields. Bowler-hatted manager Hoggard can be seen by the entrance door of the Straker.

Another superb final day image, this time of a well-illuminated Straker 8 at Thornfield, loaded with the great and good after the last official run. Bill Hardwick is the driver, while Chairman Robinson stands second from right, with Hoggard on the step behind.

A poignant lineup of the redundant fleet taken on 25 March, only one day after the abandonment. The two Ransomes, in variant liveries, can be seen on the left, with Strakers 10 and 11 on the right, and No. 3 behind. On the extreme left is Straker 6, while Thornfield House looms behind the leafless trees.

The unwanted fleet lingers on at Thornfield into the summer of 1938. In the left foreground is Straker 8, with number 4 alongside. Straker 12 can be glimpsed in the next row, with the two Ransomes in the distance. Why the latter, plus the Karriers, were not sold off for further service is anyone's guess. The vehicles eventually ended up in a local scrapyard for the derisory sum of £80 10s!

Demonstrators

Several trolleybuses were tested out under Chesterfield wires, mainly involving Leyland vehicles. In June 1928 an English Electric single-decker (CK 3898) completed 179 miles in service, probably paying its short visit while en route to Maidstone.

Pictured in front of the now-vanished Market Hall Station is the prototype lowbridge Leyland TBD1 (OV 1175), which ran nearly 5,000 miles in town between August and October 1931. This rugged-looking double-decker was later converted to petrol operation and went to Jersey in 1934. Now preserved, it has appeared at several rallies.

The big Leyland is here tested on the Brampton loop at a deserted terminus. Note the length of the trolleybooms as the vehicle manoeuvres on the turning circle.

Along High Street the newcomer pauses outside Hadfield's Pork Butchers, attracting some attention from the shoppers. Passing traffic, in the shape of the carthorse plodding stoically by, registers supreme indifference. The Leyland prototype retained the motorbus style half-cab and dummy radiator.

OV 1175 was later converted to a petrol bus, given the registration SV 6107 and is now based in Jersey, a venerable transport artefact that has survived for over eighty years. (*R. H. Symons*)

The prototype Leyland TBS1 single-decker also enjoyed an extended run in Chesterfield service in 1933, operating with the registration TJ 2822 and clocking up nearly 9,000 miles between September and December. In this scene it appears on the South Lancs system as two carefully-posed ladies appreciate its finer points.

Another Charles Hall image picks out the TBS1 on its way townwards from Whittington with Pottery Lane in the background. The tall, distant chimney belonged to a local brickworks. The land behind the conveyance now houses the new Chesterfield football stadium, opened for the 2010/11 season.

The final demonstrator, appearing in December 1935, was the magnificent TB10 six-axle double-decker, which gave Cestrefeldians the chance to experience some real luxury travel. Operating with the registration ATD 747, this advanced, two-entrance sixty-three-seater covered nearly 1,300 miles in Corporation service.

Apart from Horse Car 8, the only other preserved tram is No. 7 which, after serving as a holiday home above Two Dales over many decades, was rescued and rebuilt at Crich in the 1990s. Here, the author enjoys a trial drive on the venerable tramcar in October 1999.

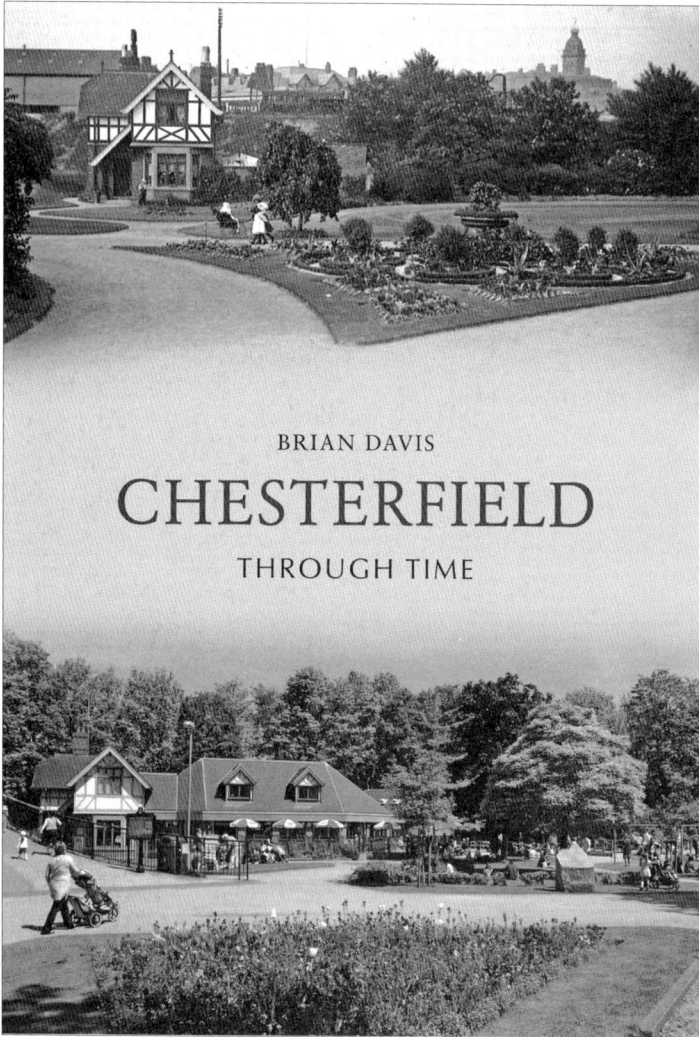